50 Breakfast Bowls Recipes for Home

By: Kelly Johnson

Table of Contents

- Avocado Toast Bowl
- Quinoa Breakfast Bowl
- Yogurt Parfait Bowl
- Smoothie Bowl
- Oatmeal Bowl
- Chia Seed Pudding Bowl
- Acai Bowl
- Egg and Spinach Bowl
- Granola Bowl
- Sweet Potato Breakfast Bowl
- Breakfast Burrito Bowl
- Banana Pudding Bowl
- Peanut Butter Banana Bowl
- Savory Quinoa Bowl
- Overnight Oats Bowl
- Fruit Salad Bowl
- Breakfast Fried Rice Bowl
- Berry Bliss Bowl
- Cottage Cheese Bowl
- Green Smoothie Bowl
- Breakfast Nachos Bowl
- Pumpkin Oatmeal Bowl
- Breakfast Couscous Bowl
- Mediterranean Breakfast Bowl
- Egg and Avocado Bowl
- Apple Cinnamon Oatmeal Bowl
- Nut Butter Bowl
- Savory Polenta Bowl
- Spinach and Feta Bowl
- Tofu Scramble Bowl
- Mexican Breakfast Bowl
- Coconut Rice Bowl
- Muesli Bowl
- Sautéed Veggie Bowl
- Maple Pecan Oatmeal Bowl

- Berry Quinoa Bowl
- Chocolate Protein Bowl
- Egg and Kale Bowl
- Blueberry Chia Bowl
- Cauliflower Rice Bowl
- Sweet and Savory Bowl
- Mediterranean Couscous Bowl
- Cinnamon Raisin Oatmeal Bowl
- Matcha Smoothie Bowl
- Zucchini Noodle Bowl
- Protein-Packed Breakfast Bowl
- Breakfast Biryani Bowl
- Almond Joy Oatmeal Bowl
- Spinach and Mushroom Bowl
- Fruity Quinoa Bowl

Avocado Toast Bowl

Ingredients

- **1 ripe avocado**
- **2 slices** whole-grain bread, toasted
- **1 tbsp** olive oil
- **Salt and pepper**, to taste
- **Red pepper flakes** (optional)
- **Sliced radishes** or **cherry tomatoes** for garnish

Instructions

1. **Prepare Avocado**: Mash the avocado in a bowl with olive oil, salt, and pepper.
2. **Assemble Bowl**: Tear or slice the toasted bread and place it in a bowl. Top with mashed avocado.
3. **Garnish**: Add radishes or cherry tomatoes and sprinkle with red pepper flakes if desired.

Quinoa Breakfast Bowl

Ingredients

- **1 cup** cooked quinoa
- **½ cup** almond milk (or milk of choice)
- **1 tbsp** honey or maple syrup
- **½ tsp** cinnamon
- **Fresh fruit** (berries, banana, etc.)
- **Nuts or seeds** for topping

Instructions

1. **Mix Base**: In a bowl, combine cooked quinoa, almond milk, honey, and cinnamon.
2. **Heat**: Microwave for 1-2 minutes until warm.
3. **Top**: Add fresh fruit and nuts or seeds before serving.

Yogurt Parfait Bowl

Ingredients

- **1 cup** Greek yogurt
- **½ cup** granola
- **1 cup** mixed berries (strawberries, blueberries, raspberries)
- **Honey**, for drizzling (optional)

Instructions

1. **Layer Ingredients**: In a bowl, layer Greek yogurt, granola, and mixed berries.
2. **Drizzle**: Top with honey if desired and enjoy!

Smoothie Bowl

Ingredients

- **1 banana**, frozen
- **1 cup** spinach
- **1 cup** almond milk (or milk of choice)
- **½ cup** frozen berries
- **Toppings**: sliced fruits, granola, nuts, seeds

Instructions

1. **Blend**: In a blender, combine banana, spinach, almond milk, and frozen berries until smooth.
2. **Serve**: Pour into a bowl and add your choice of toppings.

Oatmeal Bowl

Ingredients

- **1 cup** rolled oats
- **2 cups** water or milk
- **1 tbsp** honey or maple syrup
- **½ tsp** cinnamon
- **Toppings**: sliced bananas, nuts, dried fruit

Instructions

1. **Cook Oats**: In a pot, combine oats and water or milk. Cook according to package instructions.
2. **Mix**: Stir in honey and cinnamon.
3. **Top**: Serve in a bowl with your favorite toppings.

Chia Seed Pudding Bowl

Ingredients

- **¼ cup** chia seeds
- **1 cup** almond milk (or milk of choice)
- **1 tbsp** maple syrup
- **½ tsp** vanilla extract
- **Toppings**: fresh fruit, nuts, granola

Instructions

1. **Combine**: In a bowl, mix chia seeds, almond milk, maple syrup, and vanilla extract.
2. **Refrigerate**: Let sit for at least 4 hours or overnight until thickened.
3. **Serve**: Top with fresh fruit, nuts, and granola.

Acai Bowl

Ingredients

- **100g** frozen acai puree
- **1 banana**
- **½ cup** almond milk (or milk of choice)
- **Toppings**: granola, sliced fruits, coconut flakes

Instructions

1. **Blend**: In a blender, combine frozen acai, banana, and almond milk until smooth.
2. **Serve**: Pour into a bowl and top with granola, sliced fruits, and coconut flakes.

Egg and Spinach Bowl

Ingredients

- **2 eggs**
- **1 cup** fresh spinach
- **½ avocado**, sliced
- **Salt and pepper**, to taste
- **Olive oil**, for cooking

Instructions

1. **Sauté Spinach**: In a skillet, heat olive oil and sauté spinach until wilted.
2. **Cook Eggs**: Scramble or fry the eggs in the same skillet, seasoning with salt and pepper.
3. **Assemble Bowl**: Place spinach and eggs in a bowl, and top with avocado slices.

Enjoy your healthy bowls!

Granola Bowl

Ingredients

- **1 cup** granola
- **1 cup** yogurt (Greek or regular)
- **½ cup** mixed berries (strawberries, blueberries, raspberries)
- **Honey**, for drizzling (optional)

Instructions

1. **Layer Ingredients**: In a bowl, add a layer of yogurt, followed by granola and berries.
2. **Drizzle**: Top with honey if desired and enjoy!

Sweet Potato Breakfast Bowl

Ingredients

- **1 medium sweet potato**, cooked and diced
- **½ cup** black beans, drained and rinsed
- **1 egg**, poached or fried
- **1 avocado**, sliced
- **Salt and pepper**, to taste
- **Hot sauce** (optional)

Instructions

1. **Assemble Bowl**: In a bowl, layer the diced sweet potato, black beans, and sliced avocado.
2. **Add Egg**: Top with the poached or fried egg, seasoning with salt and pepper.
3. **Garnish**: Drizzle with hot sauce if desired.

Breakfast Burrito Bowl

Ingredients

- **1 cup** cooked brown rice
- **2 eggs**, scrambled
- **½ cup** black beans, drained and rinsed
- **½ avocado**, diced
- **Salsa**, for topping
- **Cheddar cheese**, shredded (optional)
- **Fresh cilantro**, for garnish

Instructions

1. **Combine Ingredients**: In a bowl, layer brown rice, scrambled eggs, black beans, and diced avocado.
2. **Top**: Add salsa and sprinkle with cheese if desired.
3. **Garnish**: Finish with fresh cilantro.

Banana Pudding Bowl

Ingredients

- **2 ripe bananas**, sliced
- **1 cup** vanilla pudding (store-bought or homemade)
- **½ cup** crushed vanilla wafers
- **Whipped cream**, for topping

Instructions

1. **Layer Ingredients**: In a bowl, layer banana slices, pudding, and crushed wafers.
2. **Top**: Add a dollop of whipped cream on top and enjoy!

Peanut Butter Banana Bowl

Ingredients

- **1 banana**, sliced
- **2 tbsp** peanut butter
- **½ cup** yogurt (Greek or regular)
- **Granola**, for topping
- **Chia seeds** (optional)

Instructions

1. **Assemble Bowl**: In a bowl, add yogurt, followed by banana slices and peanut butter.
2. **Top**: Sprinkle granola and chia seeds if desired.

Savory Quinoa Bowl

Ingredients

- **1 cup** cooked quinoa
- **1 cup** roasted vegetables (zucchini, bell peppers, carrots)
- **½ avocado**, sliced
- **1 egg**, poached or fried
- **Olive oil**, for drizzling
- **Salt and pepper**, to taste

Instructions

1. **Combine Ingredients**: In a bowl, layer cooked quinoa, roasted vegetables, and sliced avocado.
2. **Add Egg**: Top with the poached or fried egg, seasoning with salt and pepper.
3. **Drizzle**: Finish with a drizzle of olive oil.

Overnight Oats Bowl

Ingredients

- **1 cup** rolled oats
- **1 cup** milk (or milk alternative)
- **1 tbsp** chia seeds
- **1 tbsp** honey or maple syrup
- **Toppings**: fresh fruit, nuts, or seeds

Instructions

1. **Combine Ingredients**: In a jar or bowl, mix oats, milk, chia seeds, and sweetener.
2. **Refrigerate**: Cover and refrigerate overnight.
3. **Serve**: In the morning, top with your choice of fresh fruit, nuts, or seeds.

Enjoy your delicious breakfast bowls!

Fruit Salad Bowl

Ingredients

- **2 cups** mixed fresh fruit (berries, melon, pineapple, etc.)
- **1 tbsp** honey or agave syrup (optional)
- **1 tbsp** fresh mint, chopped (optional)
- **Juice of 1 lime**

Instructions

1. **Combine Fruit**: In a large bowl, mix together the fresh fruit.
2. **Dress Salad**: Drizzle with honey and lime juice, and toss gently.
3. **Garnish**: Add fresh mint if desired and serve chilled.

Breakfast Fried Rice Bowl

Ingredients

- **2 cups** cooked rice (preferably day-old)
- **2 eggs**, scrambled
- **1 cup** mixed vegetables (peas, carrots, bell peppers)
- **2 tbsp** soy sauce
- **1 green onion**, chopped
- **Sesame oil**, for cooking

Instructions

1. **Sauté Veggies**: In a skillet, heat sesame oil and add mixed vegetables. Cook until tender.
2. **Add Rice**: Stir in the cooked rice and soy sauce, mixing well.
3. **Add Eggs**: Push the rice to one side, scramble the eggs in the pan, then mix everything together.
4. **Serve**: Top with chopped green onion before serving.

Berry Bliss Bowl

Ingredients

- **1 cup** mixed berries (strawberries, blueberries, raspberries)
- **½ cup** yogurt (Greek or regular)
- **¼ cup** granola
- **Honey**, for drizzling (optional)

Instructions

1. **Layer Ingredients**: In a bowl, add yogurt, followed by a layer of mixed berries and granola.
2. **Drizzle**: Top with honey if desired and enjoy!

Cottage Cheese Bowl

Ingredients

- **1 cup** cottage cheese
- **½ cup** sliced peaches or berries
- **1 tbsp** honey or maple syrup
- **1 tbsp** chopped nuts (almonds, walnuts, etc.)
- **Cinnamon**, for sprinkling (optional)

Instructions

1. **Assemble Bowl**: In a bowl, add cottage cheese, then top with sliced fruit.
2. **Drizzle**: Add honey and sprinkle with nuts and cinnamon if desired.

Green Smoothie Bowl

Ingredients

- **1 banana**, frozen
- **1 cup** spinach
- **½ cup** almond milk (or milk of choice)
- **Toppings**: sliced fruits, granola, chia seeds

Instructions

1. **Blend**: In a blender, combine frozen banana, spinach, and almond milk until smooth.
2. **Serve**: Pour into a bowl and add your choice of toppings.

Breakfast Nachos Bowl

Ingredients

- **1 cup** tortilla chips
- **½ cup** scrambled eggs
- **¼ cup** black beans, drained and rinsed
- **½ avocado**, diced
- **Salsa**, for topping
- **Cheddar cheese**, shredded (optional)

Instructions

1. **Layer Chips**: Place tortilla chips in a bowl.
2. **Add Toppings**: Top with scrambled eggs, black beans, and diced avocado.
3. **Finish**: Add salsa and cheese if desired.

Pumpkin Oatmeal Bowl

Ingredients

- **1 cup** rolled oats
- **2 cups** water or milk
- **½ cup** canned pumpkin puree
- **1 tbsp** maple syrup
- **½ tsp** pumpkin pie spice
- **Toppings**: nuts, seeds, or dried fruit

Instructions

1. **Cook Oats**: In a pot, combine oats and water or milk. Cook according to package instructions.
2. **Mix in Pumpkin**: Stir in pumpkin puree, maple syrup, and pumpkin pie spice.
3. **Serve**: Top with your choice of nuts, seeds, or dried fruit.

Enjoy your delicious and nutritious bowls!

Breakfast Couscous Bowl

Ingredients

- **1 cup** cooked couscous
- **½ cup** almond milk (or milk of choice)
- **1 tbsp** honey or maple syrup
- **½ tsp** cinnamon
- **Fresh fruit** (berries, banana, etc.) for topping

Instructions

1. **Combine Ingredients**: In a bowl, mix cooked couscous, almond milk, honey, and cinnamon.
2. **Serve**: Top with fresh fruit before enjoying.

Mediterranean Breakfast Bowl

Ingredients

- **1 cup** cooked quinoa or farro
- **½ cup** cherry tomatoes, halved
- **¼ cup** cucumber, diced
- **¼ cup** feta cheese, crumbled
- **Olive oil** and **lemon juice** for dressing
- **Salt and pepper**, to taste

Instructions

1. **Assemble Bowl**: In a bowl, combine quinoa or farro, cherry tomatoes, cucumber and feta.
2. **Dress Salad**: Drizzle with olive oil and lemon juice, then season with salt and pepper.

Egg and Avocado Bowl

Ingredients

- **2 eggs**, poached or scrambled
- **1 avocado**, sliced
- **1 cup** spinach, sautéed
- **Salt and pepper**, to taste
- **Red pepper flakes** (optional)

Instructions

1. **Cook Spinach**: Sauté spinach until wilted.
2. **Assemble Bowl**: In a bowl, layer sautéed spinach, eggs, and sliced avocado.
3. **Season**: Add salt, pepper, and red pepper flakes if desired.

Apple Cinnamon Oatmeal Bowl

Ingredients

- **1 cup** rolled oats
- **2 cups** water or milk
- **1 apple**, diced
- **1 tsp** cinnamon
- **1 tbsp** maple syrup
- **Nuts or seeds** for topping

Instructions

1. **Cook Oats**: In a pot, combine oats, water or milk, and diced apple. Cook according to package instructions.
2. **Mix in Flavor**: Stir in cinnamon and maple syrup before serving.
3. **Top**: Add nuts or seeds as desired.

Nut Butter Bowl

Ingredients

- **1 cup** yogurt (Greek or regular)
- **2 tbsp** nut butter (peanut, almond, etc.)
- **1 banana**, sliced
- **Granola** for topping
- **Chia seeds** (optional)

Instructions

1. **Assemble Bowl**: In a bowl, add yogurt and swirl in nut butter.
2. **Top**: Add banana slices, granola, and chia seeds if desired.

Savory Polenta Bowl

Ingredients

- **1 cup** cooked polenta
- **½ cup** sautéed mushrooms and spinach
- **1 egg**, fried or poached
- **Grated Parmesan cheese** for topping
- **Salt and pepper**, to taste

Instructions

1. **Prepare Polenta**: In a bowl, add cooked polenta.
2. **Top**: Add sautéed mushrooms, spinach, and the fried or poached egg.
3. **Season**: Sprinkle with Parmesan cheese, salt, and pepper before serving.

Spinach and Feta Bowl

Ingredients

- **2 cups** fresh spinach
- **½ cup** cooked quinoa
- **¼ cup** feta cheese, crumbled
- **1 tbsp** olive oil
- **Lemon juice**, to taste
- **Salt and pepper**, to taste

Instructions

1. **Sauté Spinach**: In a skillet, sauté spinach until wilted.
2. **Assemble Bowl**: In a bowl, combine cooked quinoa, sautéed spinach, and feta.
3. **Dress Salad**: Drizzle with olive oil and lemon juice, seasoning with salt and pepper.

Tofu Scramble Bowl

Ingredients

- **1 block** firm tofu, crumbled
- **1 cup** mixed vegetables (bell peppers, onions, spinach)
- **1 tsp** turmeric
- **Salt and pepper**, to taste
- **Olive oil**, for cooking

Instructions

1. **Sauté Veggies**: In a skillet, heat olive oil and add mixed vegetables. Cook until tender.
2. **Add Tofu**: Stir in crumbled tofu and turmeric, cooking until heated through.
3. **Season**: Add salt and pepper, then serve in a bowl.

Enjoy your delightful breakfast bowls!

Mexican Breakfast Bowl

Ingredients

- **1 cup** cooked brown rice or quinoa
- **2 eggs**, scrambled
- **½ cup** black beans, drained and rinsed
- **½ avocado**, diced
- **Salsa**, for topping
- **Chopped cilantro**, for garnish

Instructions

1. **Assemble Bowl**: In a bowl, layer cooked rice or quinoa, scrambled eggs, and black beans.
2. **Top**: Add diced avocado and salsa, garnishing with cilantro before serving.

Coconut Rice Bowl

Ingredients

- **1 cup** cooked jasmine rice
- **½ cup** coconut milk
- **1 tbsp** honey or maple syrup
- **Fresh fruit** (mango, pineapple, etc.) for topping
- **Toasted coconut flakes** for garnish

Instructions

1. **Mix Rice**: In a bowl, combine cooked rice, coconut milk, and honey.
2. **Serve**: Top with fresh fruit and toasted coconut flakes.

Muesli Bowl

Ingredients

- **1 cup** rolled oats
- **1 cup** milk (or milk alternative)
- **½ cup** mixed nuts and seeds
- **½ cup** dried fruit (raisins, apricots, etc.)
- **Honey**, for drizzling (optional)

Instructions

1. **Combine Ingredients**: In a bowl, mix rolled oats, milk, nuts, and dried fruit.
2. **Drizzle**: Top with honey if desired and enjoy!

Sautéed Veggie Bowl

Ingredients

- **1 cup** mixed vegetables (bell peppers, zucchini, broccoli)
- **1 cup** cooked quinoa or rice
- **1 tbsp** olive oil
- **Salt and pepper**, to taste
- **Fresh herbs** for garnish (parsley, basil, etc.)

Instructions

1. **Sauté Veggies**: In a skillet, heat olive oil and add mixed vegetables. Cook until tender, seasoning with salt and pepper.
2. **Assemble Bowl**: In a bowl, layer cooked quinoa or rice and top with sautéed veggies.
3. **Garnish**: Add fresh herbs before serving.

Maple Pecan Oatmeal Bowl

Ingredients

- **1 cup** rolled oats
- **2 cups** water or milk
- **2 tbsp** maple syrup
- **¼ cup** chopped pecans
- **½ tsp** cinnamon

Instructions

1. **Cook Oats**: In a pot, combine oats and water or milk. Cook according to package instructions.
2. **Mix in Flavor**: Stir in maple syrup, pecans, and cinnamon before serving.

Berry Quinoa Bowl

Ingredients

- **1 cup** cooked quinoa
- **1 cup** mixed berries (strawberries, blueberries, raspberries)
- **½ cup** yogurt (Greek or regular)
- **Honey**, for drizzling (optional)

Instructions

1. **Assemble Bowl**: In a bowl, layer cooked quinoa, mixed berries, and yogurt.
2. **Drizzle**: Top with honey if desired and enjoy!

Chocolate Protein Bowl

Ingredients

- 1 banana
- **1 scoop** chocolate protein powder
- **1 cup** almond milk (or milk of choice)
- **1 tbsp** nut butter (peanut or almond)
- **Toppings**: sliced banana, nuts, granola

Instructions

1. **Blend**: In a blender, combine banana, protein powder, and almond milk until smooth.
2. **Serve**: Pour into a bowl and top with nut butter, sliced banana, and nuts or granola.

Egg and Kale Bowl

Ingredients

- **2 eggs**, poached or scrambled
- **1 cup** kale, sautéed
- **½ avocado**, sliced
- **Salt and pepper**, to taste
- **Olive oil**, for cooking

Instructions

1. **Sauté Kale**: In a skillet, heat olive oil and sauté kale until wilted.
2. **Assemble Bowl**: In a bowl, layer sautéed kale, eggs, and sliced avocado.
3. **Season**: Add salt and pepper before serving.

Enjoy your delicious and nutritious bowls!

Blueberry Chia Bowl

Ingredients

- **¼ cup** chia seeds
- **1 cup** almond milk (or milk of choice)
- **1 cup** blueberries (fresh or frozen)
- **1 tbsp** maple syrup or honey
- **Toppings**: sliced almonds, coconut flakes

Instructions

1. **Mix Chia Pudding**: In a bowl, combine chia seeds, almond milk, and sweetener. Stir well and let sit for at least 30 minutes or overnight.
2. **Serve**: Top with blueberries, sliced almonds, and coconut flakes.

Cauliflower Rice Bowl

Ingredients

- **2 cups** cauliflower rice
- **1 cup** mixed vegetables (bell peppers, carrots, peas)
- **1 tbsp** soy sauce
- **1 egg**, scrambled
- **Sesame oil**, for cooking

Instructions

1. **Sauté Veggies**: In a skillet, heat sesame oil and add mixed vegetables. Cook until tender.
2. **Add Cauliflower Rice**: Stir in cauliflower rice and soy sauce, cooking until heated through.
3. **Add Egg**: Push the mixture to one side, scramble the egg, and mix everything together.

Sweet and Savory Bowl

Ingredients

- **1 cup** cooked quinoa or rice
- **½ cup** roasted sweet potatoes
- **½ avocado**, sliced
- **1 fried egg**
- **Drizzle of balsamic glaze** or hot sauce

Instructions

1. **Assemble Bowl**: In a bowl, layer quinoa or rice, roasted sweet potatoes, and sliced avocado.
2. **Top**: Add the fried egg and drizzle with balsamic glaze or hot sauce before serving.

Mediterranean Couscous Bowl

Ingredients

- **1 cup** cooked couscous
- **½ cup** cherry tomatoes, halved
- **¼ cup** cucumber, diced
- **¼ cup** feta cheese, crumbled
- **Olive oil** and **lemon juice**, for dressing

Instructions

1. **Combine Ingredients**: In a bowl, mix couscous, cherry tomatoes, cucumber, and feta.
2. **Dress Salad**: Drizzle with olive oil and lemon juice before serving.

Cinnamon Raisin Oatmeal Bowl

Ingredients

- **1 cup** rolled oats
- **2 cups** water or milk
- **½ cup** raisins
- **1 tsp** cinnamon
- **Honey**, for drizzling (optional)

Instructions

1. **Cook Oats**: In a pot, combine oats, water or milk, and raisins. Cook according to package instructions.
2. **Mix in Flavor**: Stir in cinnamon and drizzle with honey if desired.

Matcha Smoothie Bowl

Ingredients

- **1 banana**, frozen
- **1 tsp** matcha powder
- **1 cup** almond milk (or milk of choice)
- **Toppings**: granola, sliced fruits, nuts

Instructions

1. **Blend**: In a blender, combine frozen banana, matcha powder, and almond milk until smooth.
2. **Serve**: Pour into a bowl and top with granola and sliced fruits.

Zucchini Noodle Bowl

Ingredients

- **2 cups** zucchini noodles (zoodles)
- **1 cup** cherry tomatoes, halved
- **¼ cup** pesto
- **Parmesan cheese**, for topping
- **Olive oil**, for cooking

Instructions

1. **Sauté Zoodles**: In a skillet, heat olive oil and add zucchini noodles. Cook for 2-3 minutes.
2. **Add Tomatoes**: Stir in cherry tomatoes and pesto, cooking until heated through.
3. **Serve**: Top with Parmesan cheese before serving.

Protein-Packed Breakfast Bowl

Ingredients

- **1 cup** Greek yogurt
- **1 scoop** protein powder (vanilla or chocolate)
- **½ cup** mixed berries
- **¼ cup** granola
- **Honey**, for drizzling (optional)

Instructions

1. **Mix Yogurt**: In a bowl, combine Greek yogurt and protein powder until smooth.
2. **Layer**: Top with mixed berries, granola, and a drizzle of honey if desired.

Enjoy your tasty and nutritious bowls!

Breakfast Biryani Bowl

Ingredients

- **1 cup** cooked basmati rice
- **½ cup** cooked chickpeas
- **½ cup** mixed vegetables (peas, carrots, bell peppers)
- **1 egg**, fried or poached
- **1 tsp** biryani spice mix (or garam masala)
- **Fresh cilantro**, for garnish

Instructions

1. **Sauté Veggies**: In a skillet, heat oil and sauté mixed vegetables until tender. Stir in chickpeas and biryani spice mix.
2. **Add Rice**: Mix in the cooked basmati rice, heating until warmed through.
3. **Serve**: Top with the fried or poached egg and garnish with fresh cilantro.

Almond Joy Oatmeal Bowl

Ingredients

- **1 cup** rolled oats
- **2 cups** almond milk (or milk of choice)
- **2 tbsp** cocoa powder
- **1 tbsp** maple syrup
- **¼ cup** shredded coconut
- **¼ cup** chopped almonds

Instructions

1. **Cook Oats**: In a pot, combine oats, almond milk, cocoa powder, and maple syrup. Cook according to package instructions.
2. **Serve**: Top with shredded coconut and chopped almonds.

Spinach and Mushroom Bowl

Ingredients

- **2 cups** fresh spinach
- **1 cup** mushrooms, sliced
- **1 cup** cooked quinoa or brown rice
- **2 eggs**, poached or scrambled
- **Olive oil**, for cooking
- **Salt and pepper**, to taste

Instructions

1. **Sauté Veggies**: In a skillet, heat olive oil and sauté mushrooms until golden. Add spinach and cook until wilted.
2. **Assemble Bowl**: In a bowl, layer cooked quinoa or rice, sautéed spinach, and mushrooms.
3. **Top**: Add poached or scrambled eggs, seasoning with salt and pepper.

Fruity Quinoa Bowl

Ingredients

- **1 cup** cooked quinoa
- **1 cup** mixed fresh fruit (berries, mango, banana)
- **½ cup** yogurt (Greek or regular)
- **1 tbsp** honey or maple syrup
- **Chopped nuts** for topping (optional)

Instructions

1. **Assemble Bowl**: In a bowl, layer cooked quinoa, mixed fruit, and yogurt.
2. **Drizzle**: Add honey or maple syrup and top with chopped nuts if desired.

Enjoy these flavorful and wholesome breakfast bowls!